The
Truth
of Me

WRITTEN WITH

EMILY MacLACHLAN CHAREST

Painting the Wind

Bittle

Who Loves Me?

Once I Ate a Pie

Fiona Loves the Night

I Didn't Do It

Before You Came

Cat Talk

Patricia MacLachlan

The Truth of Me

About a boy, his grandmother,
and
a very good dog

KATHERINE TEGEN BOOKS
An Imprint of HarperCollins Publishers

Katherine Tegen Books is an imprint of HarperCollins Publishers.

The Truth of Me
Copyright © 2013 by Patricia MacLachlan
All rights reserved. Printed in the United States of America.

Library of Congress Cataloging-in-Publication Data
MacLachlan, Patricia.
    The truth of me : about a boy, his grandmother, and a very good dog / Patricia
MacLachlan. — First edition.
        pages   cm
    Summary: Robbie and his dog, Ellie, spend the summer at his grandmother
Maddy's house, where Robbie learns many things about his emotionally distant
parents and himself.
    ISBN 978-0-06-199859-1 (hardcover bdg.)
    ISBN 978-0-06-199860-7 (lib. bdg.)
    [1. Grandmothers—Fiction.   2. Dogs—Fiction.   3. Parent and child—Fiction.]
I. Title.
PZ7.M2225Ts 2013   2012040151
[Fic]—dc23

Typography by Michelle Gengaro-Kokmen
13 14 15 16 17   CG/RRDH   10 9 8 7 6 5 4 3 2 1
❖
First Edition

For Bob

Contents

This is a true story. The truest story ever.

You may not believe it. Your loss.

But it's true.

I have a witness.

1

All About Me

My name is Robert. There are many Roberts before me—a family of Roberts. There are my uncles, my great-uncles, a grandfather and a great-grandfather, and on and on. I think of all those Roberts when I go to the ballpark and see a line of men waiting to go to the bathroom. *All those Roberts.*

I am an only child.

My parents call me Robert, and when they

do, I feel like a child dressed up in grown-up clothing. I'd rather be called Rex or Bud or Duke.

Once I asked them if they would please have another child.

My mother said, "Why would we want another child? We have you."

How dumb is that.

They did get me a dog from the shelter: a brown hound mix named Eleanor—Ellie for short. Ellie surprised us all by being obedient. She does everything we ask. Someone trained Ellie very well and then let her go. That makes me sad. Why would anyone do that?

Ellie is my best friend. Actually, Jack and Lizzie from my class are good friends, too. But they have gone to summer camp, off to swim in icy lake waters on cold mornings, to go on long hikes and forget their water bottles, to make lanyard bracelets that will unravel. They would rather go to Maddy's house with me.

So Ellie and my grandmother Maddy are my two best friends for the summer. Most kids are best friends with their dogs. Not all kids are best friends with their grandmothers. But I am.

My parents are musicians. My mother, I think, likes her violin better than she likes me. At least she spends more time with her violin than with me. But that is the way of musicians, Maddy tells me.

"That's my fault, Robbie. I gave her a quarter-size fiddle when she was seven years old to keep her from telling me what to do all the time," says Maddy.

My father (yep, named Robert) is a composer and violist. He has four pianos. There's a very big Steinway that I played under when I was little—I used to hide my glasses of milk there because I didn't like milk. The milk curdled and was cleaned up by the housekeeper much later. She never told my mother. Maybe she didn't like milk either. My father has two baby grand pianos, too, and a spinet— and a keyboard for traveling. Maddy says he is "overequipped."

Maddy calls me Robbie, which I like. And she makes my parents nervous because of the stories she tells.

I make my parents nervous, too. Which is another reason I love my grandmother.

In school we had to write a description about an actual event we witnessed. This is what I wrote about my mother auditioning a second violinist to play in her string quartet.

AUDITION OVER

The second violinist who auditions wears the same dress as the first violinist and, if you can believe it, the same shoes.

The first violinist cannot stop looking at her.

The first violinist cannot stop disliking her.

AUDITION OVER.

A tall man with a sneer auditions. He makes a grand mistake. He accuses the first violinist of being "just a trifle flat."
AUDITION OVER.

A small woman with the body of a Jack Russell terrier auditions.

She hums.

"You're humming," says the first violinist.

"I'm not."

"You are."

"I'm not."

"You are."

"I'm not."

"Are."

"Not."

"Are."

"Not."

AUDITION OVER.

My teacher, Miss Cross, laughed a lot when she read it. But she didn't think it was true. Often my teachers don't think what I write is true.

Maddy read "Audition Over" and laughed, too. But she knew it was true. She is my mother's mother, and she knows.

My parents don't exactly trust Maddy. That is, they don't trust all that she says. They whisper and murmur about her, wondering if she's going "over the edge," as my mother puts it. Once my mother called Maddy's doctor,

Henry, to tell him what she thought. I know all this because I know pretty much everything.

I know Maddy says she has lots of animal friends in the woods. I know she says she once shared corn bread with a bear, the two of them sitting on a log.

But I also know something my mother and father don't know.

Maddy has powers all her own. Powers that other people don't have.

Jack and Lizzie know this, too. They have met Maddy.

"Maddy has gifts," says Lizzie.

"Do you mean magic?" I ask.

"No. Gifts," says Lizzie. "That's different.

Remember when she was here and the birds came down from the trees to see her?"

"And a fox came?" says Jack. "It came right up to her? The animals seem to know that she is safe."

"They want to be close to her," says Lizzie. "That's her gift. They trust her."

I don't care if Maddy tells stories.

Lizzie and Jack don't care if she tells stories.

But my parents care.

And my parents are very nervous.

2

The Quirky Quartet

There is, at last, a new second violinist for my mother's string quartet. He is an unlikely choice, to look at him. He wears boots and cutoff jeans and has several tattoos on his arm, including one that says PLAY, BABY, PLAY! His name is David Chance, an interesting name since he takes a big "chance" playing with my mother. And though I can tell my mother does not approve of his clothes, her eyebrows rise with happy surprise when he begins to play.

My father is playing viola today. Marybeth, the wild-haired cellist, is going to have a baby, though you can't tell behind her cello.

My mother is annoyed with Marybeth for having a baby, I can tell. It means my mother will have to find another cellist. I think it is Marybeth's business if she wants to have a strange-looking, wild-haired baby of her own.

They are an odd bunch, I think. They are called the Allegro Quartet when they play concerts. I call them the Quirky Quartet.

The reason for the new second violinist is that the first one died in the middle of a concert, falling forward slowly into his Mozart music. That disturbed my mother's sense of how things should be. They had to stop the concert, attend to him, carry him offstage, and cancel the concert.

Today they are playing the same Mozart. They come to the soft, sweet place where the second violinist died. I suppose it is better to die in a nice, slow melody rather than a snappy one.

I almost wrote about this event for my teacher, but, for sure, Miss Cross wouldn't have believed it to be true.

They are rehearsing today in our living room before they go off on summer tour and I get to stay with Maddy. Ellie is half in love with David Chance, leaning against his leg, looking up at him as he plays.

David reaches down and scratches Ellie behind an ear, and my mother frowns. David knows she is frowning. He winks at me. He smiles brightly at my mother and plays so beautifully that she can't frown anymore.

They play and stop to talk about a note that they all hold together. Then they play again. Ellie lies down on David's foot with a sigh. She rolls over on her back. Soon, when the music reaches a crescendo, Ellie will "pass gas," as my mother puts it; and they will have to pick up their music and stands and flee to the porch to play.

Until then, Mozart and sunlight fill the room.

It is evening. A moon hangs above the meadow outside the kitchen.

My mother is on the phone.

"Yes, he's packed, Mother. We'll drive him over tomorrow. We'll be in a hurry, so we can't stop to visit."

There is a pause.

"Robert? Pick up the phone. Maddy wants to ask you a question."

She watches as I pick up the hallway phone. She doesn't hang up. I can hear her breathing.

"Robbie? Are you bringing Ellie?" asks Maddy.

"Yes," I say. "Is that all right?"

I move back in the hallway and look at my

mother, still listening on the phone. She sees me but doesn't hang up.

"Is she friendly with other animals?" asks Maddy.

"Very," I say. "She likes all dogs, and cats, and some rabbits that come around. Except for squirrels," I add. "She chases squirrels."

"We'll have to work on that," says Maddy.

Work on that?

Still my mother listens.

"I'll call you back," I say, suddenly angry.

I hang up the phone and go into the kitchen, where my mother still holds the phone. I walk up to her and take the phone out of her hand and hang it up.

"You forgot to hang up," I say to her.

17

She frowns at me, but I am used to that.

My father calls to her from the other room.

"Judith? Are you taking a case of bows?"

She turns and leaves without saying anything.

I pick up the phone and dial Maddy's
number.

"Hello?"

"It's Robbie."

"What I meant was, will Ellie be all right
with animals in the wild?" asks Maddy.

"Yes," I say, hoping that somewhere in the
house my mother is listening. My voice echoes
in the kitchen.

"Yes," I say firmly.

3

Maddy

Maddy's house sits on a hill bordered by woods.

My father drives the half-hour trip there, my mother lecturing me about "keeping watch" over Maddy.

"If she does anything strange, you can call Henry," says my mother.

Maddy always does strange things. And my parents are leaving me for two months while they go off to play. If they were really worried, they wouldn't leave me. *Would they?*

I don't say that out loud.

Henry, the town doctor, lives four houses down the road from Maddy. Maddy and Henry are friends. Better friends than my parents know. Maddy and Henry eat dinner together at least three times a week. Usually Henry cooks. Maybe this would make Henry strange to my mother, too.

I decide not to mention that to my parents.

Maddy's house looks like the house in *Little Bear*, one of my favorite books when I was little. It is a cottage with whitewashed plaster walls, big, colorful braided rugs, lots of bookshelves of books, a fireplace, and overstuffed chairs. She has a big stove, but sometimes Maddy forgets to cook supper on time. Once we had doughnuts for dinner.

I never told my parents that either. My mother and father are always cooking dishes with Swiss chard and couscous and beans and spices that are strange to me: coriander, ginger, and cloves.

There are many things that I don't tell my parents. Many things I don't say out loud. That means there are many things rolling around inside my head.

We drive into Maddy's driveway.

The car stops.

"Here," says my mother softly.

Ellie jumps out of the car first and runs

to Maddy's front door. Ellie remembers the doughnuts.

Maddy comes out, tall and thin with short, spiky white hair. She wears jeans and boots. My parents don't get out of the car. My father leans out of the window to kiss my cheek, but he doesn't hug me.

Maddy hugs me, though, and waves good-bye to my mother and father and Mozart, who is living in two big suitcases in the backseat of the car. The printed music of Mozart, that is.

Another suitcase carries some Beethoven and Schubert and some modern music I call "wikkeldy pikkeldy" music.

"We'll call," says my father.

"Don't worry, we'll have fun!" says Maddy.

"Bye, Robert!" calls my mother.

She doesn't look back when she calls to me. Her mind, I know, is already on the first concert. Then the next.

And the next.

And all the concerts after that.

"She's gone," I say out loud.

"Yes," says Maddy, understanding that I don't mean that my mother is just driving away in the car.

"She is," repeats Maddy.

Even though it is the beginning of summer there is a small fire in the stone fireplace. Maddy likes a fire. Ellie likes it, too. She edges closer and closer, stretching out on the huge bluestone hearth.

"Which room, Robbie?" asks Maddy.

There are three bedrooms downstairs and a loft upstairs that I used to choose until I got Ellie. Ellie can't climb up the ladder, and she is too big to carry.

"That one."

I point to the small room that looks over the hill going up to the woods outside. There is a high bed with a patchwork quilt.

"Can you get up there, Ellie?" I ask, patting the bed.

In a quick movement, making it look easy, Ellie leaps up onto the bed and turns around twice and lies down. She can see out of the window from the bed, and her ears stand up at something she sees.

I look out. Squirrels.

Maddy watches Ellie carefully. I know what she is thinking.

"She's a very good dog, Maddy," I say.

Maddy smiles.

"I know she is, but she *is* a hound. Hounds are known for hunting."

"She is well trained," I tell Maddy. "And she's a mix. That mix is something special, and it is why I know she will be fine in the woods." I take a breath. "With wild animals."

"And what is the mix?" asks Maddy.

"Stuffed dog," I say very seriously.

After a moment Maddy laughs for a long time.

"Okay, Robbie," says Maddy. "I trust you. I trust Ellie."

Maddy pats Ellie, and Ellie rolls over so Maddy can rub her stomach.

"I'll go pick lettuce in the garden," says Maddy, going to the kitchen. "Come on out when you want. Henry's coming for dinner tonight."

"Is Henry cooking?" I call to her.

"What do you think?" she calls back.

I stare at Ellie after Maddy leaves.

"Stuffed animal, remember," I whisper to Ellie. "I made that up," I add. "Maddy trusts you."

Ellie looks at me with her dark eyes and tilts her head.

"Maddy trusts you," I repeat, my voice sounding very serious in the little room.

I sound a little nervous, too.

I look out of the window and see Maddy in her fenced garden, picking lettuce leaves.

Why am I nervous?

Because Ellie may not be good with the wild animals of the woods?

Or because I'm afraid that there *are* wild-animal friends of Maddy's in the woods?

I sigh.

"Maybe it's easier at home with my mother and father," I say to Ellie. "At least I always know what to expect."

Ellie stares at me, her eyes big and steady and bright.

4

Small Truths

Henry comes through the doorway carrying a black cast-iron pot by its looped handle. He has a stethoscope in his jacket pocket. He is tall, with speckled hair.

"Hello, Kiddo," he says, setting the pot on the stove and turning on the gas burner.

I like Henry calling me "Kiddo."

"Hi, Henry. Did you cook that?"

Henry peers at me.

"You don't think I'd let Maddy cook, do you?"

I smile.

"She heats up doughnuts very well," I say.

Henry laughs.

I peer into the pot on the stove.

"Does this have coriander, ginger, and cloves in it?" I ask.

"No," says Henry, as if he's used to this question.

That's the nice thing about Henry. Everything you say and every question you ask he considers serious enough to answer.

Maddy says that's because he's a doctor and he is used to stupid questions from his patients.

"Where's Maddy?"

"In the shower," I say.

Henry takes the stethoscope out of his pocket and sits down at the kitchen table. He pats Ellie.

"Hello, Eleanor," he says. He always calls Ellie Eleanor.

He looks closely at me.

"All right. What?" he says.

He knows. Henry always knows when someone wants to ask a question.

"My parents called you," I say.

Henry nods.

"I heard them," I say.

Henry nods again. He sighs.

"Kiddo, your parents . . . actually, your mother thinks things should be a certain way.

Her way," he says.

I think about my mother being upset when they had to cancel a concert because the second violinist died. I think about her being upset because wild-haired Marybeth is having a baby.

I nod now. I'm turning into Henry.

"They worry about Maddy and her wild-animal stories," I say. "They think it's strange."

I'd like to say that I worry, too. But that's another thing I don't say out loud.

"We all have our truths, Kiddo," says Henry. "Some are big truths. Most times they're small truths. But those stories are Maddy's truths. Your parents have different ones of their own."

"Do you have truths of *your* own?" I ask.

"Yes," says Henry. "I am, in my heart, a man with a very large sailboat. I sail around the world with my two dogs and visit people everywhere. I like the wind in my hair. I like the sun. I like the stars at night."

I stare at Henry for a moment. For some reason, I don't know why—maybe because Henry has told me this very private thing—I feel like crying. Just so I don't cry, I ask Henry my very own stupid question.

"What kind of dogs?" I ask, my voice trembling a bit.

Henry doesn't laugh.

"Portuguese water dogs," says Henry. He takes his wallet out of his pocket and shows me a picture.

"This is what they look like."

I look at the picture of black, curly-haired dogs.

I decide to push a little more.

"And their names?"

"Are Luke and Lily," he says quickly, expecting the question.

I sit back.

Henry looks at me with a small smile.

"Do you have small truths of your own, Kiddo?" he asks.

I shake my head.

"I think I'm too young," I say.

"Oh, no. You can work on it while you're here," says Henry. "You'll have your own small truth by summer's end."

He reaches over to tap my hand. It's only a tap, but it's comforting.

"In the meantime, we won't worry about Maddy, will we?" he says in a soft voice.

"No," I whisper.

"I think we both like Maddy the way she is," says Henry.

"We do," I say.

"You have a good heart, Kiddo. Want to hear it?"

Henry picks up his stethoscope and puts the earpieces in my ears. He holds the chest piece on my chest. It is quiet in the room. Even Ellie doesn't move. And then I hear the steady *thump, thump, thump* of something inside me.

Henry knows there are tears at the corners

of my eyes, but he doesn't say so. He puts my hand over the chest piece so I can hold it there. He gets up to stir the pot on the stove.

And I sit, listening to the sound of my heart.

Listening for one small truth.

Listening to me.

Ellie and I have gone to bed.

Henry's stew was normal.

Maddy's salad was almost normal.

I can hear Henry and Maddy talking softly in the kitchen. I like the sound of their talk even though I can't hear what they say.

Ellie turns over in the dark.

I yawn.

And I realize that I'm missing something.

What is it?

I hear the quiet.

I never hear soft voices in the other room at home. And then it comes to me. What I don't hear is the sound of music. What I don't hear is the faraway sound of my mother's sweet, sad violin, the solid sound of my father playing out a melody on the piano over and over, and the sudden silence when I know he is writing it down. All that music that comes out of the night.

I close my eyes.

It is kind of nice to miss something of my mother and father.

I quickly open my eyes, surprised.

I wonder if this is a small truth.

A small truth about me.

5

Alpha

When I wake in the morning, the room is full of light.

I get up and go into the kitchen. Maddy has left a pitcher of orange juice and a glass on the table for me. I pour a glassful, then walk to the kitchen door and look out. The door is open, and I can see Maddy sitting on a wooden bench by the garden. Ellie sits at her feet.

I stop drinking my juice and put the glass

on the counter. I look again. Ellie sits, looking at Maddy. *Ellie is surrounded by squirrels.*

"Good girl, Ellie," says Maddy softly.

I come out of the house, and Maddy hears me. She holds up her hand to stop me.

"Down, Ellie," says Maddy in a kind voice.

Ellie lies down, her head on her paws. The squirrels scamper all around her, eating corn that Maddy has tossed there. One squirrel brushes against Ellie, but she doesn't move. Maddy leans down and feeds Ellie a snack.

I think about Lizzie saying that Maddy has "gifts."

I look up and see Henry standing quietly at the edge of the stone walk.

We look at each other.

Henry smiles.

I smile, too.

"How did you do that?" I ask Maddy in the kitchen. "She doesn't like squirrels at all."

"Well, some snacks," says Maddy. "Ellie likes Henry's stew. She likes the snacks more than she hates squirrels."

Ellie is prancing around proudly, as if she has done something special and heroic.

She has in a way.

"But I feed her snacks, and she always keeps chasing squirrels. Only squirrels," I point out.

"Well, I am an alpha," says Maddy.

"I'll say," Henry says.

"What is that?" I ask.

"The boss," says Henry.

"*Alpha* also means 'confidence,'" says Maddy.

"I am the leader to Ellie because I am confident I can teach Ellie not to chase squirrels. And other things," she says briskly.

Henry raises his eyebrows.

"She is right, of course," he says. "Maddy is confident."

"And Ellie likes to please people," says Maddy.

"Can I learn that?" I ask.

"I don't know," says Maddy.

"Yes," says Henry almost at the same time.

Maddy looks surprised.

"I may know Kiddo better than you do in

some ways," Henry says to Maddy.

"Really?" says Maddy.

She looks at Henry, then at me.

"Do you two have secrets?"

"No," says Henry. "Truths."

"Truths?" asks Maddy.

I nod.

"Small truths," I say.

Maddy lifts her shoulders.

"Well, then, we'll have a go at it," she says.

"What does that mean?" I ask.

"You'll see," says Maddy mysteriously. "Now, who's cooking tonight?"

"What do you have in the pantry?" asks Henry.

"Cold cereal," says Maddy.

"Oh, good grief," says Henry. "I made spaghetti sauce this morning. I'll get it."

Henry goes out the door.

"Did you make meatballs, too?" calls Maddy.

"Yes, yes, yes!" Henry calls back.

"Maddy?"

"What, Robbie?"

"You have chicken in the refrigerator," I say.

"I know," says Maddy, laughing. "I love Henry's spaghetti and meatballs."

She takes down big blue plates from the cupboard and begins to set the table. She hands me the silverware.

"Henry can roast the chicken tomorrow," Maddy whispers to me.

We look at each other over the table and begin to laugh. Ellie woofs at us happily and prances and dances, and we laugh more.

I watch Maddy make Ellie sit before she gives her a snack. I watch the way Maddy holds up her hand so Ellie will lie down.

Ellie likes following Maddy's commands. *She likes it.*

Maddy smiles at me, but she doesn't know what I'm thinking.

I tell her.

"I'm going to be an alpha, too," I say.

I put three blue napkins down next to the blue plates.

I look at Maddy.

"I am."

6

A Walk with Ellie

"I'm going to weed the garden today," says Maddy. "What are you going to do?"

"Training," I say. "I'm taking a walk with Ellie."

"I see. Training Ellie or training yourself?"

"Both."

Maddy nods.

She takes a big straw hat off the hook in the hallway and puts it on.

"Do I look like Mother Goose?" she asks.

I shake my head.

"Too thin."

"I'm going to train Ellie off leash today," I say.

"Good idea. That means she can be responsible on her own. Where are you going?"

"Henry's house."

"Be sure to remind him to roast the chicken tonight," she says as she goes out the doorway.

"Okay."

I hold the leash, and Ellie knows it. She looks at me, waiting for me to put it on her.

"No," I say. "No leash today."

I go out the doorway. When I look back, Ellie is standing there, watching me.

"Come, Ellie," I say.

Ellie comes.

Maddy is watching from the garden.

I walk down the road and Ellie walks next to me. She looks at me every so often. Every so often I tell her she's a good dog.

We walk past three houses, past a fence where there are cows. Ellie lifts her nose and sniffs the air that is their air.

"Good girl," I say.

At the end of Henry's driveway is a small white sign that says DR. HENRY BELL. Ellie and I walk up the driveway until we get to Henry's house. There is a blue door.

"This is Henry's house," I say, feeling strange telling her this. "Henry," I repeat.

The blue door opens, and Henry is there.

I wonder if Ellie thinks this is magic and me saying his name has called him out.

"Hello, Kiddo," says Henry. "Hello, Eleanor. Come in."

Ellie wags her tail but looks up at me.

"Go ahead," I say.

Ellie runs up to Henry.

We walk out of the sun into the cool of Henry's house. It is filled with books and a few paintings of boats on the sea. I walk to the back window and look out. There is a large pond there.

There is a red boat at the edge.

"Your sailboat," I say to Henry.

"My canoe," he says.

"I'm training Ellie today," I tell Henry. "So I can be an alpha."

"You're already an alpha, Kiddo," says Henry.

"What do you mean?"

"In some ways you're more alpha than your mother and father," says Henry. "Think about that."

I think about it. I don't say anything for a moment, then I remember.

"Maddy asked me to tell you to roast a chicken tonight."

Henry laughs.

"I saw that chicken yesterday," he says.

I grin at him.

"You're kind of an alpha, too," I say.

Ellie and I walk home together, no leash, Ellie close to me. Ellie doesn't chase dogs. She looks at a cat but doesn't bark or run after it. She sniffs the cows we passed before.

I lean down and kiss Ellie on her head.

I may be the very best alpha in the world.

Ellie's a good dog, too.

There's that.

It is still light when we eat Henry's roast chicken.

"So, you had a good day of training?" asks Maddy.

"I was very good," I say.

I think a bit.

"The truth is, *Ellie* was good."

Maddy nods.

"Someone taught her well when she was younger. But that doesn't mean that you aren't a good trainer, too."

Maddy doesn't own a television, but she has a small radio that is turned on. Music plays softly.

Suddenly I look up.

"Schubert," I say.

Maddy and Henry are silent.

"I know that music," I say. *"Death and the Maiden."*

I hear the sweet, sad violin. I drop my fork and get up and stand by the radio. The violin plays. The violin I know well. The violin I hear all through the days at home and into the night.

THE TRUTH OF ME

"My mother," I say very softly. "She worked hard on that piece."

Ellie comes over to stand by me. Maybe she remembers, too.

I stand there until the violin solo is finished and the quartet ends. There is applause.

The announcer's soft voice comes on, the continued sound of applause behind him.

"That was the Allegro Quartet playing Schubert's *Death and the Maiden* in London. Judith Sanders, first violin; David Chance, second violin; Robert Sanders, viola; and Marybeth Dickinson, cello."

"My mother," I say again.

Still no one speaks.

"She loves that violin," I say in a whisper.

"You can hear it."

Maddy gets up from the table and comes over to put her arms around me.

"She loves you, too, Robbie," she says. "She just doesn't know you as well as she knows that violin."

We stand there for a long time.

After a while Ellie leans against me.

7

Up the Hill
and into the Woods

Every day Ellie and I walk together, no leash. We walk up and down roads we've never walked before.

Sometimes people talk to Ellie and pat her: people walking, people in their yards. Sometimes Ellie and other dogs walking sniff noses and wag their tails. Ellie loves the attention. She even meets an escaped chicken once, and though she might want to eat that chicken, she doesn't. She looks up at me and doesn't move.

We walk to Henry's house every day.

"Henry," I say every time. "Henry."

Ellie looks at me, I think, as if to say, "I know, I know!"

Sometimes we walk down to the pond when Henry's not there. Once we sit in the red canoe and watch the summer light come through the leaves of beech trees.

My mother and father are in France now, playing quartet concerts. They haven't written yet, but I can follow them through the music sections of the newspapers. At one concert David Chance gets special praise as the new second violinist. I wonder if my mother is pleased because she chose him. Maybe. Maybe not.

My friend Jack writes me a letter.

Dear Robert,

HELP! SAVE ME! I don't like camp. We have to swim early every day in freezing water. Today I think I saw an iceberg.

Lizzie hates it, too. She fell off a horse yesterday.

Jack

Jack's letter makes me laugh out loud. It makes me happy I'm spending the summer with Maddy.

And then one morning after Ellie and I

come back from walking, Maddy has packed
up food. She has packed up water. She has
packed up a tent.

"What's happening?" I ask.

"It's time," says Maddy.

"Time?"

"To go camping," says Maddy.

Ellie sniffs the basket of food.

"You mean tonight?" I ask.

"Tonight."

"Where?"

"Up the hill and into the woods," says
Maddy.

The woods.

My nervous feeling comes back. I think

about Maddy's stories about her wild-animal friends.

"Is Henry coming?" I ask.

I know the answer.

"Of course not. Henry doesn't like to camp," says Maddy. "It's us. And Ellie."

Maddy hands me my sweater.

"It gets kind of cool at night. Ready?"

I look at Ellie, who looks right back at me as if she knows all the things I don't know.

"Okay," I say.

I pick up Ellie's leash, just in case.

Outside, Maddy puts the tent and sleeping bags and food basket in a big garden wagon with thick wheels.

"We can take turns pulling the wagon," she says.

The phone rings.

"Answer that, would you, Robbie?"

I go inside and pick up the phone.

"Hello?"

There is the thin sound of a place far away on the line. I know who it is.

"Robert?"

My mother's voice comes into my ear.

"Hello."

"How are you?" she asks.

"I'm fine."

There's a pause.

"And how's Maddy?"

"She's fine."

Another pause.

"Well, your father and I are very busy."

She sounds shy, as if talking on the phone is hard for her.

Another pause.

"I heard you play," I say.

"The Schubert?" asks Mother, suddenly more interested.

"I knew it was you," I say. "I knew the sound of your violin. I miss it," I say softly.

My mother is not interested in that.

"How did I sound?" she asks.

I close my eyes. There is silence, except for that sad sound of no one talking.

"I mean that I'm glad you knew it was me playing," says my mother suddenly, trying to be kind.

"I miss you," I say very softly.

I wait for her to say she misses me.

I wait until I realize that she's not going to say it.

"Robert?" she says.

"I can't hear you," I say. "I think the connection isn't good."

"Robert?"

Very quietly, I hang up the phone.

I go out to where Maddy waits.

"It was my mother," I say. "Let's go."

Maddy looks at me for a moment, then silently, neither of us talking, we pull the wagon up through the grasses, on a path through the woods, up to the top of the hill. Ellie noses my hand once as if to remind me she's there.

It is beautiful at the top of the hill. The sun is setting, leaving a rose sky. We set up the tent together in a clearing. Maddy builds a small campfire in a stone pit, and we eat our food. There are two logs to sit on. I stare at the logs, remembering Maddy's story about eating corn bread with a bear, both of them sitting on a log. But I don't ask Maddy about it. Ellie curls up next to the fire after she eats. The air feels good. The woods have a sweet smell.

"I don't want to talk about my mother's

call," I say to Maddy.

"Neither do I," says Maddy.

I almost smile.

When we're tired, we both go into the dome tent and go to sleep. Ellie curls up next to me, her hound body shaped to my body.

It is the next day, early morning, when the animals come.

8

The Breathing of Animals

I wake early. Maddy is still sleeping. A slice of first light comes through the tent door, but the sun hasn't come up. I put my hand over to touch Ellie. She isn't there.

Very quietly I slide from my sleeping bag and look out of the tent.

And there is Ellie, sitting quietly. Just behind her a deer and a fawn are grazing. On the log are two raccoons eating something.

A rabbit, then another, then two more come out of the woods. Chipmunks race after each other in the underbrush. Ellie sits there very silently. Once her tail wags. The animals don't seem to see her. Or if they do, they don't mind.

I slide back into the tent and touch Maddy's shoulder. She looks up right away. I don't speak, but Maddy sees me looking out of the tent. She crawls from her sleeping bag and looks, too.

"Oh, yes," she says softly. "Look at that good dog. Just look at her.

"Good work, Robbie," whispers Maddy.

"Good work, Maddy," I whisper back.

We watch for a while, then quietly come

out of the tent. I wait for the animals to run off.

But the animals stay.

I sit on the other end of where the raccoons sit, listening to them eat and chatter.

I hear the breathing of animals.

Ellie comes over for me to pat her.

The sun comes up, spreading light.

The deer raise their heads to see it.

But the animals stay.

"Want to camp again tonight?" asks Maddy.

Maddy has scrambled eggs in a black frying pan over the fire. Ellie has eaten her breakfast.

"Yes," I say.

Maddy nods and I grin.

"What's funny?"

"You're beginning to nod like Henry."

Maddy nods again.

We both laugh.

"When you spend time with people, you begin to act like them. And think like them sometimes," says Maddy.

"I plan to act and think like you," I say.

Maddy is silent.

She blinks her eyes, and I think she is trying not to cry.

Ellie gets up and stands between us, waiting for whatever food is left. The animals have gone with the sun—disappearing into the cool, dark woods.

We come off the mountain in the afternoon. We leave the tent up, with the sleeping bags inside. Maddy and I each take a handle of the food basket and walk down the hill.

"I can't wait to tell Henry about the animals," I say.

"Henry won't believe it," says Maddy. "He doesn't think it's true."

I look at Maddy for so long that she finally looks back at me over the basket.

"The truth is, Henry doesn't care if it's true," I tell her. "He told me he likes you the way you are."

This time Maddy can't blink the tears away. I pretend I don't see.

But Ellie looks up, watching Maddy. When Maddy doesn't look at Ellie, she nudges her hand with her nose. Ellie does it again. And again, until finally Maddy reaches over to stroke Ellie's head.

9

Cranky Tom

When we get to Maddy's house, Henry is sitting on the bench by the garden.

"Where have you two been?"

"Camping. We saw animals," I tell Henry. "I sat with raccoons."

Henry raises his eyebrows.

"Really."

"Really."

"The door is open," says Maddy.

"Your door is always open, Maddy. I like the sun. Do you know you have a little rabbit eating your lettuce?"

"I do," says Maddy. "That's Peter. He comes through a little space I made in the fence at the far end."

"Peter?" I say. "You mean Peter Rabbit?"

Henry and I burst out laughing.

Ellie goes over to Henry for ear scratching.

"Eleanor," says Henry.

"How's Cranky Tom?" asks Maddy.

Henry shakes his head.

"Cranky. Not good since Rufus died."

"Why don't you take Ellie over for a visit?" says Maddy.

"I see."

"Want to come?" I ask Henry.

"Of course not," says Henry, making Maddy laugh.

Henry and Ellie and I walk down the road to Tom's house.

"Raccoons?" asks Henry.

"Raccoons," I say.

We come to a small house set back from the road.

"Here we are," says Henry. "Cranky Tom's house."

We walk up the dirt driveway. Henry opens the door.

"Tom?" he calls.

Henry looks at Ellie closely for a moment, then at me.

"Would you do something for me, Kiddo?"

"Sure. What?"

"I have an old patient that I call Cranky Tom. His dog, Rufus, died two weeks ago. Tom's missing him. Would you bring Ellie to visit him? I think it would help. We can walk there."

"Sure. Ellie can make anyone feel better," I say.

"Go ahead," says Maddy. "I'll clean up and get things ready for tonight."

"What's tonight?" asks Henry.

"Camping," Maddy and I say together.

"What?"

"I've come with a visitor. Two visitors."

"I don't like visitors."

Henry smiles at me.

"You'll like these visitors," he says.

He beckons me into the house.

In the living room is a very old man, sitting in a very old chair.

"What?" says the man.

"This is Kiddo," says Henry. "Meet Tom."

"What kind of name is Kiddo?"

"It's my name for him," says Henry.

"My name is Robert," I say.

"I knew a Robert once. He was very bad."

"I'm not him," I say.

Tom laughs for a long time.

"And this is Ellie," I say.

Tom peers at Ellie, and his face changes.

"Oh, lovely. Here, Ellie."

Ellie walks over to Tom.

He scratches her behind an ear. He strokes her head.

"She has hound in her," Tom says. "Look at that beautiful face."

Tom stops patting her, and Ellie puts her head on his knees.

"Oh, nice girl," says Tom. "My dog's name was Rufus."

"Better name than Robert," I say.

Tom laughs again. Then he looks up at me.

"I miss him," he says softly.

"I would miss Ellie," I say. "Would you

like Ellie to visit you every day? We're staying at Maddy's house this summer. She's my grandmother."

"I like Maddy. I like you. And I like Ellie. That would be nice," says Tom.

I take a dog snack out of my pocket.

"You can give her this if you want. Be careful. Sometimes she thinks a finger is a snack."

Tom feeds Ellie a snack.

"Rufus always bit me by mistake," says Tom.

"We'll come again," I tell Tom.

Tom looks closely at me.

"I'd like that."

"So would I," I say. "You're not cranky at all."

Tom smiles.

"Oh, yes I am," he says.

Henry, Ellie, and I walk back to Maddy's.

"Thanks, Kiddo."

"You're welcome."

"I wanted to take his blood pressure. I knew it would go down when he was petting Ellie. But I didn't want to disturb him. Remember that. Dogs are good for your blood pressure."

I look up at Henry.

"I wish you would come camping with Maddy and me."

"Maybe someday I will."

We'd remember Henry's words later.

10

Friends

Maddy and I carry the food basket through the meadow, up the path through the woods, to the top of the hill.

Ellie jumps and twirls on the way up.

"She likes camping," I say.

"So do I," says Maddy.

"So do I," I say.

It is late afternoon, and the light is flat, coming through the trees.

"What are we eating for dinner?" I ask.

"Hamburgers," says Maddy. "I put in an ice pack. And buns and pickles and chips and sliced tomatoes and some of my baked beans with molasses. There are cookies. And corn bread," she adds quickly.

"What?" I ask.

"Corn bread," says Maddy.

"For breakfast?" I ask.

"Maybe," says Maddy.

Our tent is there in the clearing.

I unzip the flap and make sure the lantern is inside with our sleeping bags.

"Maybe we'll see shooting stars tonight," says Maddy. "I think we should sleep outside."

"You mean here? Under the sky?"

"You'll like it. It's the only way to see shooting stars. I'll start the fire. I want it to burn down so we have some nice coals for cooking."

Maddy starts a small fire and takes out the black frying pan.

The fire smells good. The woods smell good.

The light fades. Soon we'll see a sunset.

Ellie stands by the woods looking at something. Her ears go up.

"Ellie," I say quietly, the way Maddy has taught me.

Ellie sits and watches three deer—two does and a fawn—come out of the woods. They look at us. They look at Ellie. Then they walk about, eating leaves. Ellie sits down, watching them. She shakes a bit and whines.

"It's all right, Ellie," I say.

"She's not scared," says Maddy. "She's excited."

Maddy turns to look at the deer. But suddenly, as I watch, she loses her balance and falls over the log.

"Maddy!"

Maddy is lying cheekdown in the dirt and twigs. The log has rolled onto her leg. She doesn't move. I shake her arm.

"Maddy? Are you all right?"

Maddy makes a groaning sound. She tries to turn over.

"My foot," she says. "Can you lift the log off me, Robbie?"

I kneel next to her and lift the log away.

Maddy cries out.

"I'm sorry, Maddy," I say.

"It's okay. There's a pillow in the tent," she says. "Can you get it, and I can sit up against the log?"

I run into the tent and find a pillow.

I put it behind her, and I put my arms under her arms to pull her so she can lean against it.

Her face is pale.

"Can you take off my boot, Robbie?"

"Maddy, I should go get help. I should get Henry!"

"Just take off my boot," says Maddy, her

voice sounding shaky. I've never heard her voice shaky before. "My sock, too, if you can."

I undo her shoelaces. I loosen them. I pull off the boot. I try to be gentle, but Maddy cries out again. It hurts her more when I take off her sock.

And then I look up. And behind Maddy I see a black bear standing there, watching us.

I look quickly at Ellie. Her ears have gone up again. She whimpers.

"Ellie. Come. Good girl," I say as softly as I can.

Ellie growls.

"Come," I say again.

Ellie comes over to me. I hold her collar.

"Maddy," I whisper.

"I'm all right, Robbie," she says. "We'll figure this out."

"Maddy," I whisper again. "There's a bear behind you."

Maddy can't turn around to look.

"Get the corn bread," she says softly. "In the basket. Wrapped in foil."

"Can you hold Ellie's collar?" I ask.

"Yes," says Maddy.

Very slowly I go over to the basket and look inside. There is a foil package.

I carry it to Maddy.

"Unwrap it," says Maddy, her voice sounding weaker. "Put half of it away from us, where the bear can see it."

I unwrap the bread.

"Stay, Ellie," says Maddy.

"You can take the corn bread near the bear now," says Maddy.

I've never done anything in my whole life harder than what I'm doing now. I move over slowly, the bear watching me with small eyes. Such small eyes for such a bear. I put the corn bread on the ground.

I move back to Maddy. I can feel my heart beating.

"What is the bear doing?" asks Maddy.

"Sniffing," I say.

Maddy smiles a bit.

"My friend."

The bear moves in a kind of lumbering walk over to the corn bread. He lies down and eats.

I see Ellie shaking, and I reach over and hold on to her collar again.

"Ellie's shaking," I say.

"Excited," says Maddy.

"The bear is eating," I say to Maddy.

"Robbie. I can't walk. My whole leg hurts. My head hurts, too. We'll have to get Henry. You'll have to go."

It's still light out. I think of leaving Maddy, and I know I can't do that.

"No. I won't leave you."

"We have to get Henry," says Maddy.

"I know."

Maddy is sweating now.

"I'm feeling dizzy, Robbie," says Maddy.

I go into the tent and get her sleeping

bag and cover her.

"Thank you, Robbie," she says, her voice low.

And then I know what to do.

"Maddy?"

"What?"

"I'm sending Ellie," I say.

Maddy's eyes are closed.

"Ellie can do it," I say. "She knows Henry and knows how to get there."

I take a notebook and pen out of my pocket.

I write a note.

Henry,

Maddy is hurt. She can't walk. We're camping at the top of the hill. We need you.

Bring a sleeping bag.

   Kiddo

"Ellie," I whisper. "Come."

Ellie looks at me. With a small sigh, she gets up and comes over.

I take one of Maddy's shoelaces and tie the note to Ellie's collar.

I give Ellie a snack.

"Ellie. Henry. Go to Henry," I say.

Ellie looks at me. Then she looks at the bear.

"Ellie. Henry. Go now. Go!"

My voice is sounding as shaky as Maddy's voice.

But Ellie goes.

She runs down the hill a ways and turns and looks at me.

"Go. Good girl. Find Henry!" I call.

Ellie turns and runs farther down the hill, not looking back.

Soon she's out of sight.

"Henry will come," I say to Maddy.

Her eyes are closed, and she doesn't answer.

I don't like that. I want her to talk to me.

I go into the tent and get my sleeping bag.

I lie down next to Maddy and watch the bear.

I'm scared.

But it isn't the bear that scares me.

What scares me is that Maddy is hurt, and she is not talking to me.

"Maddy," I say softly.

"Yes," she says, her eyes still closed.

I'm so happy to hear her voice that I can hardly speak.

"Henry will come."

"Yes," she says, her voice faint.

I look over at the bear, still eating happily.

And then there is a movement right next to me. I turn.

It is a bobcat.

"Maddy?"

"Yes?"

"There's a bobcat. This can't be real."

"It is real, Robbie. Touch him," Maddy says in a soft voice. "He trusts me. He trusts you."

Suddenly, for a reason I don't know, I'm not scared anymore. I reach out and touch the silver side of the bobcat. I can feel his body ripple with my touch.

I lie back down next to Maddy.

"Has he ever been touched before?" I ask.

"No," says Maddy. "You're the first."

I grin. *The first! Maybe I have gifts like Maddy.*

The rabbits come as we lie there. The raccoons come and sit on the log near us.

"Friends," says Maddy softly.

Night is coming. I light the lantern, but the fire still burns.

We wait.

11

Shooting Stars

The air is cool now. But the animals are still there. Maddy is sleeping. She has no color in her face. I hear the rustling of rabbits and chipmunks. I hear the chatter of raccoons.

The sun has set.

"Maddy," I whisper.

No answer.

I hear a new sound.

Something coming.

I stand up to look.

Ellie!

Ellie stops at the clearing, waiting. She looks at the animals.

"Come, Ellie," I call to her.

She walks into the clearing.

Behind her is Henry. He carries his medical bag and a sleeping bag. He's wearing a backpack, too.

He stops, staring at the sight: the bear, the deer, the rabbits, the raccoons on a log, the bobcat.

"It's all right, Henry," I say to him.

I start to cry then.

Henry comes over and puts his arms around me. Ellie licks my hand.

The animals don't move away.

"Maddy fell over the log and hurt her foot. I took off her boot and sock."

"That's good," says Henry.

He becomes the doctor, not Henry, touching Maddy's face, putting his hand on her forehead.

"Henry?" says Maddy in a soft voice.

"I'm here," he says.

He smooths her hair.

"You came camping," she whispers.

Henry smiles at me.

"It's the pain," he says.

"She hasn't been talking. She said she felt dizzy," I say.

"Did she hit her head?"

"I think so. She said her head hurt."

He looks at the bear, who looks back at him.

Then he looks behind me.

"Is that a bobcat?" he says in a voice so soft I can hardly hear him.

"Yes."

Henry shakes his head.

"This isn't real," he says.

"That's what I said," I tell him. "But I touched him. He's real."

Henry takes a small light out of his bag.

He shines it in Maddy's eyes.

Maddy tries to brush his hands away.

He feels her head.

"She's got a bump here," he says. "But I don't think she has a concussion."

Very gently, Henry feels Maddy's foot. He moves it, and she moans.

"Can you bring the lantern closer?" he says.

I put the lantern close to Maddy's foot.

Henry feels her foot and ankle again. He sits back.

"She has a broken ankle," he says.

"Bad?"

"Bad enough. She'll have to stay off her feet for a while. I can put a temporary splint on now to keep her from moving it, but we'll have to get her off the hill to fix it properly."

"Can you wait until morning?"

"We'll have to. It's too hard to move her in the dark. Has she had water?"

I shake my head.

Henry touches my face.

"Scary, right?"

"Yes."

"We'll take care of her."

Henry takes a syringe out of his bag and pushes up Maddy's shirtsleeve. He gives Maddy a shot.

"Maddy? You'll feel better soon. I'm here. Could you get some water, Kiddo? And is there any ice? We need to keep the ankle from swelling more."

I go over to the food basket for water. I grab the ice pack.

The bear has gone now. The deer move into the woods. The bobcat still sits by the log.

His eyes shine in the dusk.

Henry builds up the fire again.

"Did you eat dinner?" he asks.

I shake my head.

"Maddy fell before we ate. You used the ice pack for Maddy, so I threw the hamburger into the woods for the animals. Maddy made baked beans."

"The beans will keep," says Henry. "I have nachos in my backpack for dinner. And cheese to melt over the fire."

Henry and I sit next to each other on the ground, leaning against one of the logs. The bobcat has gone. Maddy's eyes are closed. Her foot is propped up on the pillow I use for sleeping. Henry has made a splint.

Ellie comes over to lie down next to Henry.

"Eleanor," says Henry softly. "She found me. She pushed my front door open, and there she was."

Henry strokes Ellie's head.

"And when I didn't get up from the kitchen table, she pulled my shirt with her teeth and tore it."

"Ellie did that?"

"She wanted to let me know she hadn't just come for a visit."

"And you found the note tied to her collar?" I ask.

Henry shakes his head.

"It had fallen off," he says. "She picked it up by the front door and brought it to me."

Henry looks at me.

"That was very smart of you to send Ellie," he said.

"I couldn't leave Maddy alone. Or Ellie with . . ." I wave my hands, and Henry knows what I meant.

"With the raccoons, the rabbits, the bear, the deer, and the bobcat?"

I laugh. Henry laughs, too.

"I'm hungry," says Maddy suddenly. "And I don't think nachos are very healthy."

"The painkiller shot is working," says Henry. "And this from a woman who once served the Kiddo doughnuts for dinner," he says louder so Maddy can hear him.

He gets up and goes over to Maddy. He hands her a water bottle.

"A few sips, Maddy. You can eat in a bit, but not too much. I don't want you to get sick."

"I already feel terrible," says Maddy. "A little sicker won't hurt."

"It will, believe me," says Henry. "I'm your doctor. And a very good doctor. Listen to me."

"How will we get down the hill?" she asks.

"I'll carry you," says Henry. "It will be quite romantic."

Maddy blushes.

"I'm glad to see color in your cheeks," says Henry with a smile.

"Look!" says Maddy suddenly. "A shooting star!"

We turn and see the star cross the sky. Then another.

"I told you," says Maddy. "Didn't I say you'd see that?"

Henry sighs.

"Maddy's better," he says.

Henry melts cheese over the fire, and we spread it on nachos on paper plates. He gives Maddy a small plate.

The lantern light falls over the clearing, and the fire flickers on our faces.

"Henry?"

"What, Maddy?"

"Did you see my friends?"

Henry doesn't answer right away.

"Yes," he says finally. "I saw them."

Maddy's quiet.

"Robbie?" she says.

"Yes?"

Maddy takes a breath.

"When your mother was very little, her father went away and left us."

Henry and I look at each other.

"I never knew that," I say. "Someone should have told me that."

"I'm telling you now. She loved her father, and he just up and left. In some ways, after that, she never quite trusted people in the same way. After all, they might up and leave, too. But she had her violin. And that violin didn't let her down. She could trust that violin."

Maddy took a breath. She was getting tired again.

"What I'm trying to say is . . ." Maddy stops.

"That violin wouldn't go away," says Henry.

Maddy sighs.

"She feels safer loving her violin," says Maddy. "Do you understand, Robbie?"

"Yes," I say.

And I do.

For the rest of the night we lie in our sleeping bags—Henry on one side of Maddy and me on the other.

As the fire slowly flickers out, we watch shooting stars until we sleep.

12

The Truth of Me

The next morning Maddy's ankle and foot are still swollen and bruised.

"We'll eat what's left of the corn bread," says Henry. "Can you throw dirt on the fire, Kiddo? We need to get Maddy down the hill."

I'd heard Maddy cry out in the night once. I'd heard Henry give her water with a pill.

There are no animals today. Ellie looks for them. I look for them.

We pile everything in the garden wagon, except for the tent. I shovel dirt on the fire until I'm sure it's safe. Then I pour water over it.

"We'll come for the tent later," says Henry. "Ready?"

I pull the wagon. Henry carries Maddy.

"This will hurt you some, Maddy," he says.

"I know," she says.

Ellie walks next to me, down the path through the woods and across the meadow.

"Maddy?" asks Henry.

Maddy puts her arms around Henry's neck and her head on his shoulder. She doesn't speak.

"We're almost there," says Henry.

At Maddy's house Henry lays Maddy on her bed. He puts a pillow under her foot. Her arm is over her eyes. She doesn't move.

"I'm going to my house to get my car," he says. "It's faster that way. I'll be right back."

I watch Henry run down the road to his house.

I carry the food basket inside. I put the rolled-up sleeping bags and lantern in the hall closet.

I stand at Maddy's bedroom door and watch her. I look down and see Ellie that is standing there, too. I put my hand on her head.

I hear the sound of a car. Henry is here. Ellie goes to the kitchen door to look out. I keep watching Maddy.

Henry brushes by me into the bedroom.

"Maddy?"

"What?"

"I'm going to pick you up and carry you to the car. The passenger seat is folded back so you can lie down until we get to the hospital."

Maddy takes her arm away from her eyes.

"What about Robbie?" she says.

"I'm fine, Maddy. I'll stay with Ellie," I say.

Henry picks up Maddy as gently as he can. I move aside, and he carries her out to the car.

"I'll call you, Kiddo," he calls. "It will be a while."

He drives the car very carefully out of the dirt driveway.

And then they're gone.

We're alone in the house, Ellie and I.

I feed her and take her outside for a walk. Then we sit on the bench by the garden. We watch Peter Rabbit eat lettuce. Peter is quick and steady. He finishes one row and is starting on another. I don't stop him. Maddy has lots of lettuce.

We sit for a long time, but still Peter eats.

Birds come to sit on the fence.

The sun goes behind a cloud, then comes out again.

The phone rings, and I run inside to answer it.

"Kiddo? You all right?"

"I'm fine. Peter Rabbit has eaten two

whole rows of lettuce."

Henry laughs. I tell him that because I want to hear him laugh.

How's Maddy?"

"Fine. She's getting a better splint. She'll get a cast in a few days. I'm bringing her home later."

I don't talk for a minute. I *can't* talk. And I know it is because I have been scared.

"Kiddo?"

"I'm fine. I'm happy she's coming home."

"Me, too."

"Henry?"

"Yes?"

"I was scared."

"Me, too," says Henry.

Maddy comes home with crutches, but Henry won't let her walk with them. He carries her into the kitchen.

"Bed or chair?" he asks.

"Chair," says Maddy until she sits down. "Bed," she says. "I'm too tired."

"Good choice," says Henry. "You have lots of medicine in you, too. You might slide down to the floor and become a rug."

I laugh.

Henry puts Maddy on her bed and comes into the kitchen.

He sits at the kitchen table.

"I'll stay here tonight," says Henry. "In case Maddy needs help."

"That's good."

The phone rings and I answer.

"Hello."

"Robert?"

My mother.

"Hello."

"Your father and I have been thinking that we need to spend some more time with you," she says. "Our last conversation wasn't very satisfying."

"No," I say. "It wasn't."

Henry looks at me. He knows who it is the way he knows all things.

"And we thought maybe you could come to London and spend time here while we're playing concerts. We could arrange for you to

111

fly over. How does that sound?"

I wait a second. And in that second I see my mother as a very young child after her father had left her. I never thought about her as a very young child before. Ever.

"Mother, Maddy has broken her ankle and is on crutches. She needs me. She has taken care of me so far. I'm going to stay and take care of her."

There is a hollow, empty sound on the phone.

"Is she all right?"

"Yes. Henry is taking care of her. She tripped in the garden."

Henry smiles at me.

"I didn't get to tell you how good you

sounded when you played the Schubert," I say. "I listened to *Death and the Maiden* on Maddy's radio."

"Well, thank you, Robert. That's so nice."

My mother is surprised. She doesn't know what else to say. She doesn't know how to talk about us: about how we feel, how we think, and how we are sometimes scared.

But I do.

I want to say many things.

I want to say that I know many new truths about myself.

I want to say I am an alpha and Ellie is a hero.

I want to say I have fed corn bread to a bear who did not hurt me.

I want to say I have touched a bobcat.

I want to say I know my mother was a small child who was lonely and sad.

But I can't say all these things.

But there is one thing I can say.

So I say it.

"Mother?"

"Yes, Robert?"

The telephone wire hums. We are both close and faraway at the same time.

"I love you," I say.

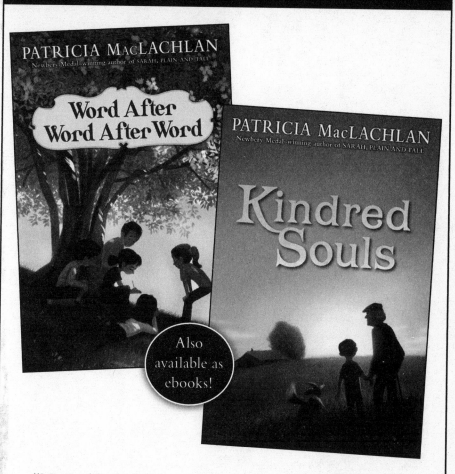